Dear Friend,

Journaling is one of our favorite things to do, and we hope it becomes one of yours, too. Journaling simply means writing down your thoughts, your feelings, and the things that are going on in your life.

The blessings of journaling are many. Sometimes, when you feel confused or frustrated, journaling can actually help you figure out what you think or feel. Journaling is also a way of writing your own history. When you look back on what you've written—weeks or years from now—you will be amazed to see how God has worked in your life and how you have grown. Journaling can be a form of prayer to God, if you want it to be. Writing out your prayers, instead of trying to say them in your head as you're falling asleep at night, is an excellent way to stay focused, and it provides you with a record to see how God answers your prayers over time.

This journal has been created with you in mind. The first two pages allow you space to write about yourself. The next four give you some ideas of things you might write about, and all the other pages are yours to write on to your heart's content!

Our prayer is that God bless and keep you as you grow in Him.

About Me

This journal belongs to _____

I received it on _____ from_____

I am _____ years old.

I go to school at_____

The best thing about school is _____

_____

My favorite subjects and classes are _____

_____

My sports/hobbies/activities are _____

_____

_____

_____

_____

I go to church at_____

The best thing about my church family is _____

_____

My best friend(s) is (are) _____

_____

_____

You are the only girl like you in all of the world,
so don't try to be like someone else.—Terry

The best thing about being this age is _____

_____

_____

My favorite TV shows are _____

_____

My favorite music groups are _____

_____

My favorite celebrities are _____

_____

On the weekends I love to _____

_____

My favorite Bible verses are _____

_____

My plans and dreams for the future are _____

_____

_____

_____

_____

_____

_____

_____

_____

Fix your thoughts on what is true and honorable and right.
Think about things that are pure and lovely and admirable.—Philippians 4:8

girls of grace

Date_____ Day_____ Time_____

The weather today was_____

What's up with my friends?_____

_____

_____

_____

_____

_____

_____

_____

_____

What's up with my family?_____

_____

_____

_____

_____

_____

_____

_____

Have confidence that if you have done a little thing well,
you can do a bigger thing well too.—Terry

Boys! Boys! Boys! What's going on? _____

_____

_____

_____

_____

_____

_____

_____

_____

_____

What's up in my spiritual life? (Bible verses I read and what I
learned from them; prayer requests and answers) _____

_____

_____

_____

_____

_____

_____

_____

_____

Whatever you do, work at it with all your heart, as working for the Lord, not for men....
It is the Lord Christ you are serving.--Colossians 3:23-24

The best part of today was _____

_____

_____

_____

_____

_____

_____

_____

The worst part of today was _____

_____

_____

_____

_____

_____

_____

Tomorrow I look forward to _____

_____

_____

_____

_____

_____

Sometimes God just wants me to be still and get to know Him.—Heather

People and things that helped me today: _____
_____
_____
_____
_____
_____
_____

What I did to help someone else: _____
_____
_____
_____
_____
_____
_____
_____
_____

My "to-do" list:

_____   _____
_____   _____
_____   _____
_____   _____
_____   _____

✿ When it comes to makeup, less is more.

Date_____ Day_____ Time_____

_____

_____

_____

_____

_____

_____

_____

_____

_____

_____

_____

_____

_____

_____

_____

_____

_____

_____

_____

_____

_____

_____

The good news is that God is always pursuing you
—and He will never stop.—Denise

Therefore, if anyone is in Christ, he is a new creation; the old has gone,
the new has come!—2 Corinthians 5:17

Date _____ Day _____ Time _____

_____

_____

_____

_____

_____

_____

_____

_____

_____

_____

_____

_____

_____

_____

_____

_____

_____

_____

_____

If all we do is talk,
not many people will want to be around us.--Terry

Man looks at the outward appearance, but the Lord looks at the heart.—1 Samuel 16:7

_____

_____

_____

_____

_____

_____

_____

_____

_____

_____

_____

_____

_____

_____

_____

_____

_____

_____

_____

_____

_____

_____

_____

_____

_____

What I thought was a total pain,
I now see was for my own good.—Heather

In all things God works for the good of those who love Him,
who have been called according to His purpose.—Romans 8:28

girls of grace

Date _____ Day _____ Time _____

_____

_____

_____

_____

_____

_____

_____

_____

_____

_____

_____

_____

_____

_____

_____

_____

_____

_____

_____

_____

_____

Before you date a guy,
pray about it and tell God how you feel.—Denise

_____

_____

_____

_____

_____

_____

_____

_____

_____

_____

_____

_____

_____

_____

_____

_____

_____

_____

✿ Get ready early—rushing stresses you out. Set your alarm clock to wake you up 20 minutes earlier than your current wake-up time.

girls of grace

Date_____ Day_____ Time_____

_____

God has given us a beautiful gift in sex,
but He firmly restricts it to marriage.—Denise

Marriage should be honored by all, and the marriage bed kept pure,
for God will judge the adulterer and all the sexually immoral.—Hebrews 13:4

girls of grace

Date _____ Day _____ Time _____

_____

_____
_____
_____
_____
_____
_____
_____
_____
_____
_____
_____
_____
_____
_____
_____
_____
_____
_____
_____
_____
_____

Hear me when I say: A good friend does not talk harmfully
about a friend behind her back.—Terry

✿ To soothe razor burn, either soak in chamomile tea
or apply tea bags to irritated area.

Date_____ Day_____ Time_____

A soft, sweet reply or turning the other cheek
will work wonders.—Shelley

Let your conversation be always full of grace, seasoned with salt,
so that you may know how to answer everyone.—Colossians 4:6

Date_____ Day_____ Time_____

_____

_____
_____
_____
_____
_____
_____
_____
_____
_____
_____
_____
_____
_____
_____
_____
_____
_____
_____
_____
_____
_____
_____
_____

Prayer is more than asking God for things—
prayer is also about getting to know God.—Heather

Look to the Lord and His strength;
seek His face always.—Psalm 105:4

girls of grace

Date_____ Day_____ Time_____

_____

_____

_____

_____

_____

_____

_____

_____

_____

_____

_____

_____

_____

_____

_____

_____

_____

_____

_____

_____

_____

_____

_____

_____

_____

_____

_____

_____

If we put on the mind of Christ in our relationships,
imagine how much more we would care for others.—Denise

_____

_____

_____

_____

_____

_____

_____

_____

_____

_____

_____

_____

_____

_____

_____

_____

_____

_____

_____

✿ Never sleep in your makeup. If you'll take it off right after school and put on a light moisturizer, you'll be ready for bed hours early!

Date________ Day________ Time________

When a brother or sister is nagging or bothering you,
let your first thought be love.—Shelley

For if you forgive men for their transgressions,
your heavenly Father will also forgive you.—Matthew 6:14

girls of grace

Date_____ Day_____ Time_____

_____

_____

_____

_____

_____

_____

_____

_____

_____

_____

_____

_____

_____

_____

_____

_____

_____

_____

_____

_____

_____

_____

Unconditional forgiveness is the key to any relationship.—Terry

✿ Curl your eyelashes to make your eyes look bigger and brighter.

girls of grace

Why is it that we fight with our siblings,
but we're so utterly concerned about getting along with our friends?—Shelley

Each of you should look not only to your own interests,
but also to the interests of others.—Philippians 2:4

Date_____ Day_____ Time_____

_____

_____

_____

_____

_____

_____

_____

_____

_____

_____

_____

_____

_____

_____

_____

_____

_____

_____

_____

_____

_____

_____

_____

_____

Make sure you are looking for love
in the right place.—Denise

A true friend is skilled in the art of listening.—Terry

Everyone should be quick to listen, slow to speak and slow to become angry.—James 1:19

When you confess your sins to God,
be as specific as you possibly can.—Heather

✿ To help remind yourself to drink water,
use bottles of water and count how many you drink each day.

girls of grace

Date_____ Day_____ Time_____

_____

_____

_____

_____

_____

_____

_____

_____

_____

_____

_____

_____

_____

_____

_____

_____

_____

_____

_____

_____

_____

_____

_____

Don't place yourself in situations that you know
have a strong chance for a bad outcome.—Denise

Bad company corrupts good character.
—1 Corinthians 15:33

I didn't drink or do drugs, but I did have a famously smart mouth.—Shelley

Speak the truth with love.—Ephesians 4:15

girls of grace

Date _____ Day _____ Time _____

_____

Learn the art of giving unselfishly,
and you will truly be happy.—Terry

✿ Makeup only looks as good as your skin underneath;
so take good care of your skin.

girls of grace

Date _____ Day _____ Time _____
_____

The Bible is God's thoughts to us.
—Heather

All Scripture is inspired by God and profitable for teaching, for reproof, for correction, for training in righteousness.—2 Timothy 3:16

Date_____ Day_____ Time_____

_____

_____

_____

_____

_____

_____

_____

_____

_____

_____

_____

_____

_____

_____

_____

_____

_____

_____

_____

_____

_____

_____

_____

Immerse yourself in God's love and accept His forgiveness.—Denise

✿ Lipstick does not have to be the exact shade of your clothing, but it should not clash.

girls of grace

Date_____ Day_____ Time_____

_____

God is weaving all the circumstances of your life into a gorgeous tapestry.—Shelley

I trust in God's unfailing love for ever and ever.—Psalm 52:8

Date_____ Day_____ Time_____

When I journal, I tell God my thoughts and
dreams and fears and successes.—Heather

✿ If you want to look slimmer, don't wear horizontal stripes—
they focus the eye to your width.

Be encouraging, and you will be trusted and well liked.—Terry

Encourage one another daily, as long as it is called Today.—Hebrews 3:13

Date _____ Day _____ Time _____

_____

_____

_____

_____

_____

_____

_____

_____

_____

_____

_____

_____

_____

_____

_____

_____

_____

_____

_____

_____

_____

Through all the good and bad of our lives,
God is making us more like Jesus.—Shelley

✿ Sunscreen is a must—it is the best thing you can do
to keep your skin beautiful year-round!

It's never too late to make things right.
—Denise

✿ Check out your local beauty school for super-cheap manicures and pedicures.

girls & grace

Date _____ Day _____ Time _____

_____

_____
_____
_____
_____
_____
_____
_____
_____
_____
_____
_____
_____
_____
_____
_____
_____
_____
_____
_____
_____
_____
_____
_____

Laughter is medicine to your soul.—Terry

A cheerful heart is good medicine, but a crushed spirit dries up the bones.—Proverbs 17:22

Love does not demand its own way.—Denise

✿ Too tight is too wrong. No matter how great your body is, tight clothes pull funny.

girls of grace

Date_____ Day_____ Time_____

_____

_____

_____

_____

_____

_____

_____

_____

_____

_____

_____

_____

_____

_____

_____

_____

_____

_____

_____

_____

_____

_____

_____

_____

Spending time in His Word is a key ingredient
to keeping yourself pure.--Heather

I have hidden Your Word in my heart,
that I might not sin against You.—Psalm 119:11

girls of grace

Date_____ Day_____ Time_____

_____

_____

_____

_____

_____

_____

_____

_____

_____

_____

_____

_____

_____

_____

_____

_____

_____

_____

_____

_____

_____

_____

By obedience, I mean being a big enough person to accept what your parents say
and obey them whether you agree or not.—Shelley

✿ Wear clothing that best flatters your figure.
You don't have to follow the current trends if it is not best for you.

Date_____ Day_____ Time_____

The one thing that never changed in all my years of journal entries
is the presence of God.—Heather

Then you will call upon Me and come and pray to Me,
and I will listen to you.—Jeremiah 29:12

girls of grace

Date_____ Day_____ Time_____

_____

_____
_____
_____
_____
_____
_____
_____
_____
_____
_____
_____
_____
_____
_____
_____
_____
_____
_____
_____
_____
_____
_____
_____
_____

Work at being sensitive to the feelings of others,
even if it is not natural for you.—Terry

Tomorrow I look forward to...

✿ Don't spend too much time looking at yourself in the mirror.
Doing so will make minor flaws seem huge.

girls of grace

Date_____ Day_____ Time_____

_____

What's up with my friends?

With God's help, you can be pure
in the way you think and the way you act.—Denise

How can a young person stay pure?
By obeying Your Word and following its rules.—Psalm 119:9

In reality, obedience
is our *only* option.—Shelley

People and their love stories

❁ When tweezing, remove hairs one at a time and pull in the direction of the hair growth.

_____

_____

_____

_____

_____

_____

_____

_____

_____

_____

_____

_____

_____

_____

_____

_____

_____

_____

_____

_____

_____

You can actually make a plan for who you want to become
and set out to become that person.—Terry

When there are many words, transgression is unavoidable,
But he who restrains his lips is wise.—Proverbs 10:19

girls of grace

The way to "know Jesus better" is by reading and studying the Bible.—Heather

✿ Store lipstick and perfume in the refrigerator—they will last longer.

Date_____ Day_____ Time_____

_____

_____

_____

_____

_____

_____

_____

_____

_____

_____

_____

_____

_____

_____

_____

_____

_____

_____

_____

_____

God loved you so much that He sent His Son
to die for your sins.—Denise

For God so loved the world that He gave His one and only Son,
that whoever believes in Him shall not perish but have eternal life.—John 3:16

girls of grace

Date_____ Day_____ Time_____

_____

_____

_____

_____

_____

_____

_____

_____

_____

_____

_____

_____

_____

_____

_____

_____

_____

_____

_____

_____

_____

God knows all about you and your heartaches.—Shelley

✿ To avoid lipstick on your teeth, after application,
run your finger through the middle of your lips and pull back out.

Girls of Grace

Date _____ Day _____ Time _____

_____

_____
_____
_____
_____
_____
_____
_____
_____
_____
_____
_____
_____
_____
_____
_____
_____
_____
_____
_____
_____
_____
_____
_____
_____

What seemed like the hugest deal when I was thirteen
is absolutely meaningless now.—Shelley

A gentle answer turns away wrath,
but a harsh word stirs up anger.—Proverbs 15:1

Date_____ Day_____ Time_____

_____

I don't know about you, but I need God daily.—Heather

✿ Rinse your hair in cold water after shampooing to make hair extra shiny.

girls of grace

Date _____ Day _____ Time _____

_____

_____

_____

_____

_____

_____

_____

_____

_____

_____

_____

_____

_____

_____

_____

_____

_____

_____

_____

_____

_____

_____

Our focus needs to be on coming closer to God
in all our relationships.—Denise

But seek first His kingdom and His righteousness,
and all these things will be given to you as well.—Matthew 6:33

God doesn't call us to be average teenagers,
but to live our lives by a higher standard.—Shelley

_____

_____

_____

_____

_____

_____

_____

_____

_____

_____

_____

_____

_____

_____

_____

_____

_____

_____

_____

_____

_____

_____

✿ Be careful about mixing patterns. The combinations you see in magazines
are put together by professionals.

girls of grace

Date_____ Day_____ Time_____

_____

_____

_____

_____

_____

_____

_____

_____

_____

_____

_____

_____

_____

_____

_____

_____

_____

_____

_____

_____

_____

Use your head, and don't give in to peer pressure.
—Terry

Let your light shine before men, that they may see your good deeds
and praise your Father in heaven.—Matthew 5:16

Date_____ Day_____ Time_____

_____

_____

_____

_____

_____

_____

_____

_____

_____

_____

_____

_____

_____

_____

_____

_____

_____

_____

_____

_____

_____

_____

_____

Many of the best guy-girl relationships
are friendships.—Denise

Somehow I look forward to...

✿ Create a balance with makeup. If you give yourself dramatic eyes,
then use soft lip color and vice versa.

God delights in you, and His plan is for you to delight in Him.—Heather

Delight yourself in the LORD and He will give you the desires of your heart.—Psalm 37:4

girls of grace

Date_____ Day_____ Time_____

_____

_____
_____
_____
_____
_____
_____
_____
_____
_____
_____
_____
_____
_____
_____
_____
_____
_____
_____
_____
_____
_____

Our friend Jesus will help us through any
and every thing life sends our way.--Shelley

_____

_____

_____

_____

_____

_____

_____

_____

_____

_____

_____

_____

_____

_____

_____

_____

_____

_____

_____

_____

✿ One pound of muscle burns 150 calories a day,
while a pound of fat burns only 3. Resistance training builds muscle.

True friends see others through the eyes of God.—Terry

✿ Get at least eight hours of sleep a night to keep your skin looking fresh.

Some of my very best memories are times spent with friends.—Terry

A friend loves at all times, and a brother is born for adversity.—Proverbs 17:17

My life has been a bit of a roller coaster, and most of the ups and downs
are written in the pages of my journals.—Heather

✿ For super-soft feet, scrub them with a grainy exfoliant right before going to bed, then slather with tons of Vaseline and sleep with socks over the Vaseline.

Date_____ Day_____ Time_____

_____

_____

_____

_____

_____

_____

_____

_____

_____

_____

_____

_____

_____

_____

_____

_____

_____

_____

_____

_____

When dating, set boundaries and plan ahead.—Denise

Listen to advice and accept instruction, and in the end you will be wise.—Proverbs 19:20

girls of grace

Date _____ Day _____ Time _____

_____

_____

_____

_____

_____

_____

_____

_____

_____

_____

_____

_____

_____

_____

_____

_____

_____

_____

_____

_____

_____

I could have served my sister by sharing some of my "precious" time
simply playing with her.—Shelley

✿ To prevent lipstick from fading, apply foundation to lips
before applying lipstick.

girls of grace

Date_____ Day_____ Time_____

_____

_____
_____
_____
_____
_____
_____
_____
_____
_____
_____
_____
_____
_____
_____
_____
_____
_____
_____
_____
_____
_____
_____

It's not how many friends we have that matters,
but the precious qualities of those friends.—Terry

Be kind to each other, tenderhearted, forgiving one another.
—Ephesians 4:32

girls of grace

Date_____ Day_____ Time_____

_____

_____

_____

_____

_____

_____

_____

_____

_____

_____

_____

_____

_____

_____

_____

_____

_____

_____

_____

_____

_____

_____

_____

_____

_____

_____

There is something very freeing
about writing your thoughts to God.—Heather

_____
_____
_____
_____
_____
_____
_____
_____
_____
_____
_____
_____
_____
_____
_____
_____
_____
_____
_____
_____
_____
_____
_____
_____

Pray in the Spirit on all occasions
with all kinds of prayers and requests.—Ephesians 6:18

girls of grace

Date_____ Day_____ Time_____

_____

_____

_____

_____

_____

_____

_____

_____

_____

_____

_____

_____

_____

_____

_____

_____

_____

_____

_____

_____

_____

_____

Stop and think before
you blurt out your thoughts.—Terry

Date _____ Day _____ Time _____

_____

_____

_____

_____

_____

_____

_____

_____

_____

_____

_____

_____

_____

_____

_____

_____

_____

_____

_____

_____

_____

_____

Train yourself to take time to think and pray before you react.—Shelley

If any of you lacks wisdom, let him ask of God, who gives to all men generously and without reproach, and it will be given to him.—James 1:5

Date_____ Day_____ Time_____

_____

You can read a psalm a day for five months.
—Heather

✿ Wear makeup to enhance your best features.
Don't draw attention to your makeup, but to your face.

_____

_____

_____

_____

_____

_____

_____

_____

_____

_____

_____

_____

_____

_____

_____

_____

_____

_____

_____

_____

_____

_____

We were created for fellowship with God, and prayer is a beautiful way
to have that fellowship with Him.—Heather

Love is patient, love is kind.
—1 Corinthians 13:4

girls of grace

Date_____ Day_____ Time_____

_____

_____

_____

_____

_____

_____

_____

_____

_____

_____

_____

_____

_____

_____

_____

_____

_____

_____

_____

_____

_____

_____

_____

_____

Sometimes we have a hard time believing that God loves us in spite of our sin.
But He does.—Denise

✿ Avoid tanning. Instead, choose a good sunless tanning lotion
to get that sun-kissed look.

Date _____ Day _____ Time _____

_____

_____
_____
_____
_____
_____
_____
_____
_____
_____
_____
_____
_____
_____
_____
_____
_____
_____
_____
_____
_____
_____

The inner beauty of your heart and soul will shine farther
than any outer beauty ever could.—Terry

_____

_____

_____

_____

_____

_____

_____

_____

_____

_____

_____

_____

_____

_____

_____

_____

_____

_____

_____

_____

Charm is deceitful and beauty is vain, but a woman who fears the Lord,
she shall be praised.--Proverbs 31:30

girls of grace

Date_____ Day_____ Time_____
_____

_____
_____
_____
_____
_____
_____
_____
_____
_____
_____
_____
_____
_____
_____
_____
_____
_____
_____
_____
_____
_____
_____

Having an adult friend you can trust is important.
—Denise

✿ When accessorizing, balance is the key. If you go heavy on the accessories, keep clothes simple, and vice versa.

Love the Lord your God with all your heart and with all your soul
and with all your mind.—Matthew 22:37

Our purpose at Howard Publishing is to:

- *Increase faith* in the hearts of growing Christians
- *Inspire holiness* in the lives of believers
- *Instill hope* in the hearts of struggling people everywhere

Because He's coming again!

Girls Of Grace Journal © 2002 by Point Of Grace
All rights reserved. Printed in the United States of America

Published by Howard Publishing Co., Inc.
3117 North 7th Street, West Monroe, Louisiana 71291-2227

04 05 06 07 08 09 10 11   10 9 8 7 6 5

Edited by Philis Boultinghouse
Interior design by Stephanie Denney
Cover design by LinDee Loveland

ISBN-13: 978-1-4516-4148-6